ABUNDANT TRUTH INTERNATIONAL MINISTRIES

Abundant Truth Leadership Series

Keys to Apologetics

Exploring the Mandate, the Mindset, and the Method of Christian Apologetics

Roderick Levi Evans

Keys to Apologetics

Exploring the Mandate, the Mindset, and the Method of Christian Apologetics

All Rights Reserved. © 2025 Roderick L. Evans

No part of this book may be reproduced or transmitted in any form or by any means, graphic, electronic, or mechanical, including photocopying, recording, taping or by any information storage or retrieval system, without the permission in writing from the publisher.

Front & Back Cover Designs by Abundant Truth International Publishing
Image by Arnie Bragg from Pixabay

Abundant Truth Publishing
an imprint of Abundant Truth International Ministries

For information address:
Abundant Truth International
P.O. Box 126
Camden, NC 27921

ISBN: 978-1-60141-650-6

Printed in the United States of America

Unless otherwise indicated, all of the scripture quotations are taken from the *Authorized King James Version* of the Bible. Scripture quotations marked with NIV are taken from the *New International Version* of the Bible. Scripture quotations marked with NASV are taken from the *New American Standard Version* of the Bible. Scripture quotations marked with Amplified are taken from the *Amplified Bible*.

Contents

Introduction

Chapter 1 - The Mandate of Apologetics   1

The Search for Truth   *3*
The Foundation of Apologetics   *5*
The Definition of Apologetics   *7*

Chapters 2 - The Mindset of Apologetics   15

Fading Traditionalism   *17*
Formulating Mindset   *18*

Chapter 3 – The Method of Apologetics   25

Discovering the Method   *27*

Contents (cont.)

Discovering the Mentality   29

Chapter 4- Basic Apologetics for Apologists[4]   35

Key Verses on Apologetics   37

Bibliography   63

Introduction

God anoints and endows individuals with gifts and talents to serve in the Church. However, some have missed the very purpose of gifts and ministries in the Church. In the Abundant Truth Leadership Series, we will endeavor to present a proper foundation for believers to minister upon.

In this publication

The publication brings emphasis to the conviction that Christian apologetics is a responsibility for all believers, not just a select few.

It begins with a personal relationship with Jesus and the presence of the Holy Spirit.

Apologetics involves defending the faith with meekness and fear, as mandated by Peter in his first letter. Christians must be prepared mentally and spiritually to defend their faith, especially in an age of relativism.

-Chapter 1-

The Mandate of Apologetics

KEYST TO APOLOGETICS

Exploring the Mandate, the Mindset, and the Method of Christian Apologetics

What is truth? This question posed by Pilate to Jesus has challenged philosophers, thinkers, and theologians.

The Search for Truth

However (like Pilate who walked away after his inquiry) many who claim they are in search of truth really have no interest in finding "truth" because it will demand a lifestyle response.

Therefore, many make truth elusive, especially where the divine is concerned, so no ultimate commitment or rejection is required due to glorified agnosticism.

Though there have been distortions of the Christian faith, doctrine, and practice, the core truth claims of Christianity remain.

The Christian, today, has to be willing to stand on the faith and have the proper approach, appeal, and apparatus to defend the faith.

This chapter begins our

discussion concerning Christian apologetics among believers.

The Foundation of Apologetics

When individuals hear the word apologetics, they oftentimes feel this is reserved for a special class of Christians who are well versed, educated, and hold some sort of ecclesiastical accreditation or office.

However, anyone who has received Christ is capable of engaging in apologetics. Apologetics does not begin with study, research, knowledge of Hebrew and Greek, or a comprehensive understanding of Church history (all of which are important and will enhance one's ability as an apologist).

However, it starts with a personal relationship with Jesus Christ through the indwelling presence of the Holy Spirit.

A personal encounter with the Christ serves as the Christian's initial evidence of the reality of the truth of God revealed in Christ. It is the basis for all true apologetics.

The Definition of Apologetics

Now, the question remains, what is apologetics? Apologetics comes from a Greek word meaning "speaking in defense." It is not complicated in its scope.

Every Christian who has received Christ should be able to speak in defense of their faith and hope in Him.

Each individual will be unique in how they approach defending the faith. Some will do it in scholarly settings and debates while others will defend the faith among family, friends, and the community.

It is a charge that is laid upon all who have received God's gracious gift of salvation.

It is not something to be afraid of. If you have received Him and know the gospel message, you have the necessary tools to stand as a Christian apologist.

In his first letter, Peter gives his

readers the mandate for speaking in defense of the faith; again, to stand as Christian apologists.

> *But sanctify the Lord God in your hearts: and be ready always to give an answer to every man that asketh you a reason of the hope that is in you with meekness and fear: Having a good conscience; that, whereas they speak evil of you, as of evildoers, they may be ashamed that falsely accuse*

your good conversation in Christ. I Peter 3:15-16

This call to be able to defend the faith extends to Christian today. We cannot be afraid to say that there is one truth which is revealed in Christ. In an age of relativism, to assert that there is one truth that is seemed as bigotry, ignorance, and arrogance.

However, we cannot allow cultural criticism to hinder our kingdom witness. On today, ask Christ for grace, strength and wisdom to stand in defense of the faith. In the next two chapters, we will from the above verses, explore how to engage in apologetics.

In the next chapter, we will discuss "The Mindset of Apologetics." Until then, remain faithful to Him who will never leave you nor forsake you.

KEYST TO APOLOGETICS
Exploring the Mandate, the Mindset, and the Method of Christian Apologetics

KEYST TO APOLOGETICS

Exploring the Mandate, the Mindset, and the Method of Christian Apologetics

Notes

KEYST TO APOLOGETICS

Exploring the Mandate, the Mindset, and the Method of Christian Apologetics

_____

_____

_____

_____

_____

_____

_____

-Chapter 2-
The Mindset of Apologetics

KEYST TO APOLOGETICS

Exploring the Mandate, the Mindset, and the Method of Christian Apologetics

Relativism is an established doctrine of today's society.

Fading Traditionalism

Though there are those who hold to traditional values with respect to culture and religion, the global trend is to promote the idea of "personal truth."

This means that what is true for one, may not be true for another: just live out your own truth.

Because of this prevailing attitude toward faith and spirituality, the Christian must be spiritually and mentally prepared to engage in apologetics. The Christian must have the proper mindset while standing in defense of the faith.

Formulating Mindset

Continuing our examination of I Peter 3:15-16, we find that Peter gives us the proper mindset needed for effective apologetics.

> *"...but sanctify Christ as Lord in your hearts, always being ready to make a defense to everyone who asks you to give an account for the hope that is in you..."* (I Peter 3:15a)

As opposed to the generalized theism presented in society, the Christian has to have a passionate, unwavering fear, reverence, and respect for the Christian faith and the

Lord of that faith, Jesus.

Peter commanded that the Lord be sanctified in their hearts. The greek word used for "sanctify" here means to make holy or consecrate.

If Jesus is not considered the only true person of worship, then the Christian will not see the need to defend the truth of God revealed in Christ.

Moreover, if they do, it will be for the sake of lively conversation rather than an appeal to the listener to receive Christ as the only way of salvation.

In addition to Christ being sanctified in the believer's heart, Peter admonished them to be ready to give an answer. The Christian has to be, in effect, "on standby."

Regardless of the day or hour, they are mentally prepared to defend their faith with a reasonable argument, fueled by their hope of eternal life. The Christian's mindset has to be governed by these exhortations of Peter to present an effective witness of Jesus Christ.

In our next chapter, we will look more specifically at the method and/or manner that one should adhere to while in defense of the faith.

KEYST TO APOLOGETICS

Exploring the Mandate, the Mindset, and the Method of Christian Apologetics

Notes

KEYST TO APOLOGETICS

Exploring the Mandate, the Mindset, and the Method of Christian Apologetics

-Chapter 3-

The Method of Apologetics

A common expression is, "There is a method to the madness." Though this expression is used to defend someone's unorthodox ways to accomplish certain tasks.

It partially holds true for apologetics; namely, there is a method to defending the faith.

Discovering the Method

In our first two chapters, we briefly addressed the mandate and the mindset of apologetics, respectively.

However, there is a method to do this from a biblical perspective.

The method to apologetics does not begin in following prescribed steps, but in the internal approach of the one engaging in it.

Continuing our examination of I Peter 3;15-16, we find these words,

> *"...with meekness and fear: fear: Having a good conscience; that, whereas they speak evil of*

you, as of evildoers, they may be ashamed that falsely accuse your good conversation in Christ." (I Peter 3:15b-16)

Discovering the Method

Peter admonished the believers to be ready to defend the faith, but the method to be employed is meekness and fear. This means that the believer should boldly declare their faith out of a reverence of God and in an unoffensive manner.

Though people will be offended by what the Christian may say, the Christian's character should not be called into question due to erratic, irrational, and demeaning behavior as they defend the faith.

Peter tells them that meekness and fear is needed as to not give the opposing side a valid reason to malign the believer personally as an attempt to not hear their message.

We see today that Christians have

been guilty of not defending the faith in meekness and fear. Some have been highly offensive and ungodly in their approach.

Again, when we speak of offensive, we mean using derogatory and demeaning language to expose sin and ungodliness.

We can stand on the truth boldly without resorting to ungodly tactics to make the biblical position clear.

Remember, the goal of apologetics is not to win a debate or argument, but to give individuals a clear presentation of the gospel, that they, peradventure, will enter into a relationship with the Lord Jesus Christ.

Notes

-Chapter 4-

Basic Apologetics for Apologists

KEYST TO APOLOGETICS

Exploring the Mandate, the Mindset, and the Method of Christian Apologetics

Here is a list some verses and various passages that show the apologetic ministry and discipline was vibrant and active in the early New Testament Church.

Key Verses on Apologetics

1 Peter 3:15-16 *"But in your hearts revere Christ as Lord. Always be prepared to give an answer to everyone who asks you to give the reason for the hope that you have. But do this with gentleness and respect,* *keeping a clear conscience, so that those who speak maliciously against your good behavior in Christ may be ashamed of their slander."*

2. Jude 3 *"Dear friends, although I was very eager to write to you about the salvation we share, I felt compelled to write and urge you to contend for the faith that was once for all entrusted to God's holy people."*

3. Titus 1:9 *"He must hold firmly to the trustworthy message as it has* *been taught so that he can encourage others by sound doctrine and refute those who oppose it."*

4. 2 Timothy 2:24-26 *"And the Lord's servant must not be quarrelsome but must be kind to everyone, able to teach, not resentful. Opponents must be gently instructed, in the hope that God will grant them repentance leading them to a knowledge of the truth, and that they will come to their senses and escape from the trap of the devil, who has taken them captive* to do his will."

5. Jude 22 *"Be merciful to those who doubt..."*

6. Luke 7:19-22 *"When the men came to Jesus, they said, "John the Baptist sent us to you to ask, 'Are you the one who is to come, or should we expect someone else?'" At that very time, Jesus cured many who had diseases, sicknesses, and evil spirits, and gave sight to many who were blind. So he replied to the messengers, "Go back and report to John what you* *have seen and heard: The blind receive sight, the lame walk, those who have leprosy are cleansed, the deaf hear, the dead are raised, and the good news is proclaimed to the poor. Blessed is anyone who does not stumble on account of me."*

7. Isaiah 48:5 *"Therefore I told you these things long ago; before they happened I announced them to you so that you could not say, 'My images brought them about; my* *wooden image and metal god ordained them."*

8. Acts 19:8-10 *"Paul entered the synagogue and spoke boldly there for three months, arguing persuasively about the kingdom of God. But some of them became obstinate; they refused to believe and publicly maligned the Way. So Paul left them. He took the disciples with him and had discussions daily in the lecture hall of Tyrannus. This went on for two years so that all the Jews and*

Greeks who lived in the province of Asia heard the word of the Lord."

9. Acts 18:27-28 *"When Apollos wanted to go to Achaia, the brothers and sisters encouraged him and wrote to the disciples there to welcome him. When he arrived, he was a great help to those who by grace had believed. For he vigorously refuted his Jewish opponents in public debate, proving from the Scriptures that Jesus was the Messiah."*

10. 2 Corinthians 10:5 *"We demolish arguments and every pretension that sets itself up against the knowledge of God, and we take captive every thought to make it obedient to Christ."*

Apologetics is a major way of doing spiritual warfare. It's being able to deconstruct arguments and pretentious arguments that trip people up and keep them out of the kingdom.

11. Colossians 2:8 *"See to it that no one takes you captive through hollow and deceptive philosophy, which depends on human tradition and the elemental spiritual forces of this world rather than on Christ."*

12. Luke 1:1-4 *"Many have undertaken to draw up an account of the things that have been fulfilled among us, just as they were handed down to us by those who from the first were eyewitnesses and servants of the word.*

13. 2 Peter 1:16 *"For we did not follow cleverly devised stories when we told you about the coming of our Lord Jesus Christ in power, but we were eyewitnesses of his majesty."*

14. 1 John 1:1-3 *"That which was from the beginning, which we have heard, which we have seen with our eyes, which we have looked at and our hands have touched—this we proclaim concerning the Word of life. The life appeared; we have seen it and testify to it, and we proclaim to you the* *eternal life, which was with the Father and has appeared to us. We proclaim to you what we have seen and heard, so that you also may have fellowship with us."*

15. 1 Corinthians 15:3-8 *"For what I received I passed on to you as of first importance: that Christ died for our sins according to the Scriptures, that he was buried, that he was raised on the third day according to the Scriptures, and that he appeared to Cephas, and then to the Twelve. After* *that, he appeared to more than five hundred of the brothers and sisters at the same time, most of whom are still living, though some have fallen asleep. Then he appeared to James, then to all the apostles, and last of all he appeared to me also, as to one abnormally born."*

16. Romans 1:18-20 *"The wrath of God is being revealed from heaven against all the godlessness and wickedness of people, who suppress the truth by their wickedness since* *what may be known about God is plain to them, because God has made it plain to them. For since the creation of the world God's invisible qualities— his eternal power and divine nature— have been clearly seen, being understood from what has been made, so that people are without excuse."*

17. Psalm 19:1-4 *"The heavens declare the glory of God; the skies proclaim the work of his hands. Day after day they pour forth* speech night after night they reveal knowledge. They have no speech, they use no words; no sound is heard from them. Yet their voice goes out into all the earth, their words to the ends of the world."

18. Colossians 4:5-6 *"Be wise in the way you act toward outsiders; make the most of every opportunity. Let your conversation be always full of grace, seasoned with salt, so that you may know how to answer everyone."*

19. Philippians 1:16 *"...I am put here for the defense of the gospel."*

20. Mark 12:12-37 And they sought to lay hold on him, but feared the people: for they knew that he had spoken the parable against them: and they left him, and went their way.

And they send unto him certain of the Pharisees and of the Herodians, to catch him in his words.

And when they were come, they say unto him, Master, we know that thou art true, and carest for no man: for thou regardest not the person of men, but teachest the way of God in truth: Is it lawful to give tribute to Caesar, or not?

Shall we give, or shall we not give? But he, knowing their hypocrisy, said unto them, Why tempt ye me? bring me a penny, that I may see it.

And they brought it. And he saith unto them, Whose is this image and superscription? And they said unto him, Caesar's.

And Jesus answering said unto them, Render to Caesar the things that are Caesar's, and to God the things that are God's. And they marvelled at him.

Then come unto him the Sadducees, which say there is no resurrection; and they asked him, saying,

Master, Moses wrote unto us, If a man's brother die, and leave his wife behind him, and leave no children, that his brother should take his wife, and raise up seed unto his brother.

Now there were seven brethren: and the first took a wife, and dying left no seed.

And the second took her, and died, neither left he any seed: and the third likewise.

And the seven had her, and left no seed: last of all the woman died also.

In the resurrection therefore, when they shall rise, whose wife shall she be of them? for the seven had her to wife.

And Jesus answering said unto them,

Do ye not therefore err, because ye know not the scriptures, neither the power of God?

For when they shall rise from the dead, they neither marry, nor are given in marriage; but are as the angels which are in heaven.

And as touching the dead, that they rise: have ye not read in the book of Moses, how in the bush God spake unto him, saying, I am the God of Abraham, and the God of Isaac, and the God of Jacob?

He is not the God of the dead, but the God of the living: ye therefore do greatly err.

And one of the scribes came, and having heard them reasoning together, and perceiving that he had answered them well, asked him, Which is the first commandment of all?

And Jesus answered him, The first of all the commandments is, Hear, O Israel; The Lord our God is one Lord:

And thou shalt love the Lord thy God with all thy heart, and with all thy soul, and with all thy mind, and with all thy strength: this is the first commandment.

And the second is like, namely this, Thou shalt love thy neighbour as thyself. There is none other commandment greater than these.

And the scribe said unto him, Well, Master, thou hast said the truth: for there is one God; and there is none other but he:

And to love him with all the heart, and with all the understanding, and with all the soul, and with all the strength, and to love his neighbour as himself, is more than all whole burnt offerings and sacrifices.

And when Jesus saw that he answered discreetly, he said unto him, Thou art not far from the kingdom of God. And no man after that durst ask him any question.

And Jesus answered and said, while he taught in the temple, How say the scribes that Christ is the Son of David?

For David himself said by the Holy Ghost, The LORD said to my Lord, Sit thou on my right hand, till I make thine enemies thy footstool.

David therefore himself calleth him Lord; and whence is he then his son? And the common people heard him gladly.

KEYST TO APOLOGETICS

Exploring the Mandate, the Mindset, and the Method of Christian Apologetics

Notes:

Bibliography

Smith, William. *Smith's Bible Dictionary.* Holman Bible Publishers. Nashville, TN. c1994

The Bible Library. *The Bible Library CD Rom Disc.* Ellis Enterprises Incorporated, (c) 1988 – 2000. 4205 McAuley Blvd., Suite 385, Oklahoma City, OK 73120. All Rights Reserved.

Lockman Foundation. *Comparative Study*

Bible. Zondervan Publishing House. Grand Rapids, MI, c1984

Manning, Erik (2018). 19 Essential Bible Verses and Passages on Apologetics that Every Christian Should Know. *https://isjesusalive.com/19-bible-verses-on-apologetics/. Is Jesus Alive.*

Notes:

KEYST TO APOLOGETICS
Exploring the Mandate, the Mindset, and the Method of Christian Apologetics

Notes: